Contents

KU-619-060

An economic catastrophe

A crowd in New York's Wall Street at the time of the Great Crash, 29 November 1929.

In early September 1929, the prices of **shares** on the **Wall Street stock market** in New York, which had been rising steadily for seven long years, began to slip backwards. Not a lot, but enough to make some people nervous. Then prices began to inch back upwards, which reassured everyone. It was just a rocky patch, the buyers told each other. Soon prices would resume their relentless, and wonderfully profitable, rise.

The Wall Street Crash

However, in late October the slip turned into a slide. A sudden wave of selling on Saturday 19 October carried over into the following week, driving prices down and eventually causing panic selling on 'Black Thursday', 24 October. Nearly 13 million shares changed hands on that day, most of them at prices far below the sellers' worst nightmares. The buyers, who thought they were scooping up bargains, would find themselves in the same dreadful situation only days later.

Over the weekend several of the largest banks tried to halt the slide by buying shares, but by now confidence in the market had all but evaporated. Rumours of catastrophe were everywhere. The rush to sell was on, and nothing could stop it. Monday was bad, but 'Black Tuesday', 29 October, was the worst day of the 'Great Crash'. The American economist J. K. Galbraith called it 'the most devastating day in the history of markets'. Over 16 million shares were sold, many for practically nothing. Thousands of individual investors, and hundreds of companies which had been set up to **invest** for others, were ruined.

WALL STREET STOCK MARKET

THIS WAS THE PLACE WHERE **STOCKS** AND SHARES IN AMERICAN BUSINESSES WERE BOUGHT AND SOLD. SHARES WERE CERTIFICATES REPRESENTING PIECES OF THE BUSINESS, WHICH ENTITLED THE HOLDER TO A SHARE OF ANY PROFITS. COMPANIES SOLD SHARES IN THEMSELVES TO FINANCE THEIR OPERATIONS. THE VALUE OF SHARES FELL DRAMATICALLY IN 1929, AS THESE FIGURES SHOW. (ALL FIGURES ARE IN US DOLLARS):

	MAR 28	SEP 29	NOV 29
GENERAL ELECTRIC	129	396	168
GENERAL MOTORS	140	182	36
WOOLWORTH	181	251	52

Men who had driven expensive limousines and dined in New York's fanciest restaurants became beggars overnight, and there was a wave of suicides in New York's financial district. It is said that the clerks of one hotel even started asking new guests whether they needed a room for sleeping or jumping.

It soon became clear that investors were not going to be the only people to lose their livelihoods and savings as a result of the Great Crash. As the American government did nothing, refusing even to attempt to correct the situation, the tentacles of collapse spread outwards from Wall Street, across America, across the oceans, until there was hardly a family on earth which was left unaffected.

The effects of the Great Crash were felt world-wide. This march of the unemployed took place in Germany.

The Great Depression

Banks and companies went under, dragging others down with them, both in the US and abroad. The world economy shrank in on itself. As firms all over the world went **bankrupt**, or desperately cut back their costs to save themselves from bankruptcy, so another wave of jobs disappeared, until it seemed as if jobs were being sucked by the million into an economic black hole of terrifying dimensions.

That black hole came to be known as the Great Depression. It lasted longer in some countries than in others, but for several years in all of them. It dominated the period between the two world wars, blighting millions of lives with poverty and hopelessness. It was at least partly responsible for the rise of **Nazism** in Germany, and for World War Two (1939–1945). It would colour the way most people thought about the relationship between economics and politics for the rest of the 20th century, and still haunts us today.

It was heartbreaking

*I must have gotten calls from a dozen and a half friends who were desperate. In each case, there was no sense in loaning them the money that they would give the **broker**. Tomorrow they'd be worse off than yesterday. Suicides, left and right, made a terrific impression on me, of course. People I knew. It was heartbreaking … On Wall Street, the people walked around like zombies. It was very dark. You saw people who yesterday rode around in Cadillacs lucky now to have car fare.*

A Wall Street financier in October 1929

Consequences of World War One

World War One ended in November 1918, but its impact on the world economy would be felt for many years. The death of so many millions, the ruination of large areas of Europe, the triumph of **communism** in Russia – each would have economic consequences. So too would the less obvious changes, like the distortion of normal trade patterns and the changing balance of economic power between the richer nations.

The distance of the USA and Japan from the war in Europe had given their economies a chance to grow. Others, like the British and French, had gone deep into debt to pay for the war, and the German economy had been badly bent out of shape by the strain of continuing the struggle. One important economy – the Russian – had been virtually removed from the world economy by revolution and civil war. All across the world some industries had been artificially encouraged by the needs of the war, while others, less necessary to the war effort, had struggled to survive.

If the post-war world economy was to prosper and grow, it needed time to adapt to all these changed circumstances. The first requirement was a fair and lasting peace.

Stability proves hard to achieve

There were several reasons why this proved impossible to achieve. The victorious nations were less interested in fairness than in grasping the spoils of victory. They wanted to see their victory reflected in new borders, and over the next few years many changes were made, often with little regard for the wishes of the people who actually lived in the regions concerned. This short-sighted policy encouraged a rash of minor disputes in the 1920s, and in later years would provide the German leader Adolf Hitler with the excuses he needed to set out on a policy of conquest. The new **League of Nations**, which US President Woodrow Wilson hoped would help to settle such disputes, was fatally weakened when his own country refused to join.

There were many casualties in World War One. These soldiers are learning to walk using artificial legs, 1919.

The victorious nations also decided to demand financial compensation from the losers. These **reparations** would mostly have to be paid by an already weakened Germany. In the **Treaty of Versailles**, signed in 1919, a 'war guilt clause' stated that Germany had been completely responsible for starting the war, and a huge figure – £6.6 billion – was set. The economist John Maynard **Keynes**, who attended the Versailles Conference as a member of the British delegation, resigned in disgust over this issue. Germany could not pay such an amount, he wrote, and making her do so would create an economic disaster. The world economy would be unbalanced still further.

This political and economic instability was made worse by the lack of economic leadership. The USA had replaced Great Britain as the most powerful player in the world economy, but American political and economic leaders were reluctant to take on any global responsibilities. They did not think it necessary. After all, most economists at this time thought that economies did best when the politicians left them alone. The world economy in 1918–20 was like a broken bone, they thought – it just required time to re-knit itself. Few realized that the bone had been pushed so far out of shape by the war that surgery was needed if it was ever to heal properly.

Not the only guilty party

We are required to admit that we alone are war guilty. Such an admission on my lips would be a lie.

Senior German delegate at Versailles

David Lloyd George, Georges Clemenceau and Woodrow Wilson at the Versailles Peace Conference, 1919.

Ten-pin bowls

The world's economies were now so interconnected that trouble in one meant trouble in others. The Americans might wish to keep out of European quarrels, and the British and the French might be happy to see Germany in ruins, but when it came to economic matters they were all more dependent on each other and the rest of the world than ever before. National economies were like ten-pin bowls – a direct strike on one was likely to bring down others. A direct strike on the lead pin – the USA – could bring them all down.

Europe in the 1920s

The most powerful European nations had suffered greatly from the war, but each also had its own particular problems. In Britain a short post-war **boom** ended abruptly in the winter of 1920–1. Higher taxes and a cutback in government spending left less money in people's pockets, and businesses found it harder to find buyers for their goods and services. Economic growth slowed dramatically, and unemployment doubled in the four months to March 1921. Wages fell and industrial disputes became more frequent. This was not the 'country fit for heroes', promised by wartime **propaganda**, although **unemployment insurance** was extended to cover most of the working population.

French troops during their occupation of the Ruhr in Germany, January 1923.

France had suffered more in the war. More men had been killed and maimed, and large areas of the north had been laid waste by the fighting. As in Britain, French governments tried to promote stability by **balancing their budgets**. It was hard to raise taxes in France. The upper and middle classes blocked the raising of **direct taxes**, which would hit them hardest, and the working classes blocked the raising of **indirect taxes**, which would have cost them more. French governments were left to rely on the expected German **reparations** to make up the shortfall.

Crisis in Germany

Germany, virtually brought to her knees by the strain of the war, was forced to agree the huge reparations demand from the victorious allies. The first instalment of £2 billion was paid in gold, iron, coal and timber shipments, but when the second one was due there were not enough goods left to meet it. The French refused to accept that the Germans could not pay, and in 1923 their troops occupied Germany's richest area – the industrial Ruhr valley – intending to simply take what was owed. The Germans responded by refusing to work or cooperate with the invaders.

This enraged the French, but also created the conditions for a complete collapse in Germany. The Ruhr was now producing nothing, and many more workers were looking to the government for support.

Germany's great inflation

In 1923 I was advertising chief of a rubber factory. That was during the inflation. I had a monthly salary of 200 billion marks. We were paid twice a day, and then everybody had a half-hour's leave so that he could rush to the stores and buy something before the next quotation on the dollar came out, at which time the money would lose half its value.

A character in the German author Erich Maria Remarque's novel of 1938, *Three Friends*

Children in Germany playing with worthless money during the Great Inflation of 1923.

The politicians tried to make up the difference by printing money, and an already inflationary situation spiralled out of control. A loaf of bread which cost two-thirds of a mark in 1918, and 250 marks in January 1923, cost 201 billion marks by November of that year. German money had become virtually worthless.

Such a situation was clearly not in anyone's interests. If the Germans could not pay reparations to the British and French, they in turn would not be able to pay off their war debts to the USA. So over the next year a financial deal, the Dawes Plan, was worked out. The USA would loan Germany enough money to rebuild its economy and pay reparations to France and Britain. These countries would then be able to pay their debts.

A hopeful period

At first this arrangement proved very successful. In Europe, the years between 1925 and 1929 were marked by growing prosperity and increasing political stability. In many countries unemployment remained high, and the threat of **inflation** still persisted, but the overall economic picture seemed to be brightening at last. Only a few people knew how dependent the whole European economy was on the health of the American economy. Stresemann, the German Foreign Minister, was one of them. 'Germany is in fact dancing on the edge of a volcano,' he said in 1929. If the Americans demanded the repayment of their loans, he added, then a large section of the German economy would collapse.

The USA in the 1920s

During World War One the American economy had expanded to fill the gap left by lower production of many goods in Europe. Once the war was over this **demand** fell away, and for a brief period the economy went into **recession**. These difficulties were one cause of the social unrest which followed the war. In 1919–20 there were race riots, and disputes among workers in the police, and in the coal and steel industries. A great fear of **communist** influence in the USA created a 'Red Scare'. Thousands of people were arrested, mostly for short periods.

The Ford assembly line at Dearborn, Michigan, March 1928.

A booming economy

Warren Harding became president in 1921, the first of three successive **Republican** presidents. Over the next eight years he and his successors – Calvin Coolidge (1923–9) and Herbert Hoover (1929–33) – followed policies which favoured business. Income tax and taxes on business were reduced, **indirect taxes** raised. It became easier to borrow money. **Tariffs** on industrial **imports** were also raised, protecting American industry from outside competition.

These policies created an industrial **boom**, which was reinforced by the growth of new industries based on technological progress. The motor industry was the most important. Its expansion helped fuel the growth of other industries – like steel, rubber and glass – whose products were used in the construction of cars. There was also a vast growth of the household appliance industry, as families rushed to buy the new refrigerators, radios and vacuum cleaners. For many Americans this was a time of steadily increasing prosperity. Workers' pay doubled during the decade.

Of course, not everyone shared in this prosperity. The farmers, helped by new agricultural technology, were producing too much, and prices for their crops remained low. The Republicans' pro-business policies, though good at encouraging growth, were also widening the gap between rich and poor, and the poorest Americans, many of whom belonged to ethnic minorities, were having a hard time making ends meet.

Black Americans set up groups to campaign for reform. They asked the government for help in improving their general situation. They also asked for laws against **lynching** and new voting rights. The requests were ignored.

A dangerous optimism

For the majority of Americans, the 1920s were a time of great optimism. The decade became known as the 'roaring 20s', the 'age of excess', the 'jazz age'. There were all the new gadgets, the first flights across oceans, films with sound, the new rhythm music. The world was changing so fast, and all for the better. There seemed no reason why prosperity should ever end, no limit to what Americans could achieve, or own, or do.

The man who put the 'jazz' into 'jazz age'. Louis Armstrong with his band, 'Hot Five', in 1925.

As the decade went by this sense of optimism encouraged two dangerous states of mind. One was the feeling that nothing could go wrong, and that therefore nothing had to be done to guard against disaster. The president's 1928 State of the Union address, (see box) was a good example of this. The second state of mind was a sort of wild blindness, a willingness to take what, in any other time, would have been considered foolish chances. The best example of this was the mad rush to make money through gambling on the stock market.

Official optimism

No Congress of the United States ever assembled, on surveying the state of the Union, has met with a more pleasing prospect than that which appears at the present time. The great wealth created by our enterprise and industry, and saved by our economy, has had the widest distribution among our own people, and has gone out in a steady stream to serve the charity and business of the world. The requirements of existence have passed beyond the standard of necessity into the region of luxury. The country can regard the present with satisfaction and anticipate the future with optimism.

From President Coolidge's State of the Union address, 1928

The Great Crash

The Florida land boom

The widespread belief that every American could now get rich received its first setback in the Florida land **boom** of 1924–6. Land in Florida was very cheap at the beginning of the decade, but as the state grew more popular for holidays and retirement homes, the price began to rise. Buyers of property in Florida only had to come up with 10 per cent of the price for a 'binder', a piece of paper giving them the exclusive right to buy that piece of land. When the value of the land went up they could sell this 'binder' and make a big profit, without ever needing to pay the other 90 per cent.

This system worked well, and everyone made a profit, as long as the price of Florida land kept rising. However, by 1926 most of the good land had been sold, a hurricane had done great damage to the state, and prices had begun to fall. Those at the end of the chain, who had paid over-high prices for binders, found that they owed 10 per cent of the price on land which was now worth much less than the 10 per cent they had already paid out.

Up, up and away

Another version of the same sad story would be repeated a few years later on the **Wall Street stock market**. The price of a **share** was supposed to reflect the well-being of a company. If it was a big company, with high expected profits, then generally the price of the shares would be high. But such calculations were often hard to make exactly, and other factors – from rumours to the health of the economy as a whole – could influence share prices.

If it was expected that prices would keep on rising, then some people would buy shares just to sell them again a little later and pocket the profit. These people, who were not interested in the long-term health of the companies whose shares they bought, were more like **speculators** than investors. In America in the late twenties confidence was so high, and the chances of growing rich by gambling on the stock exchange so good, that a fever of speculation took hold.

Things were made easy for the speculators. As with land in Florida, people were allowed to buy with a 10 per cent deposit. In the stock market it was called buying 'on the margin'. In addition, investment **trusts** were formed which sold shares in themselves and used the money they received to buy other shares, often in other investment trusts. There were 300 of these trusts in 1927, and 750 only two years later. The price of shares kept going up, but each day the price bore less and less relation to anything in the real world of work and production.

The bubble bursts

In that world, there were signs as early as 1928 that the boom was coming to an end. The farmers were still in trouble, and the widening gap between rich and poor was now affecting industrial production. By this time the rich had bought all the new appliances they needed, and there were too many poor people who could not afford to buy any. Since the rest of the world had responded to American **tariffs** with tariffs of its own, the surplus American goods could not be sold overseas.

It was only a matter of time before this economic downturn began to raise doubts about the price of shares. The first doubters sold their shares, and, slowly at first, but soon with dizzying speed, the fever of buying turned into a fever of selling. In a few days in October 1929 the stock market on Wall Street came crashing down. By mid-November it had lost 40 per cent of its value and many thousands of investors had lost everything.

Panic in Wall Street following news of the Crash, 29 October 1929.

They were the first victims of this man-made disaster, but far from the last. Over the next few years there would be millions more, and they would be found in almost every country on the planet.

From Crash to Depression

Historians and economists have argued about the relationship between the Great Crash and the Great Depression. All agree that it was not a simple matter of one causing the other. The existing depression was partly to blame for the **stock market** crash, but the crash was then responsible for the depression turning out much deeper and longer than it would otherwise have been.

It may seem strange that a collapse of prices on the stock market could have such a huge impact on the rest of the economy. After all, only about four million people (out of an American population of over 100 million) owned **shares**, and fewer than half that number were serious players on the stock exchange. But the rippling effects of the Crash were soon spreading across America, bringing disaster in their wake. Weaker businesses were swept away, and even some of the strongest had trouble surviving.

The collapse of confidence

The first thing the Great Crash destroyed was confidence. No one wanted to risk **investing** in an economy which was on the slide; on the contrary, most people were desperate to get back any money they had already invested while that was still possible. The same was true of simple bank deposits. Many banks had lost heavily in the stock market crash, and the customers of all banks were now eager to take out their money at the first hint of trouble. It only needed one person to start a run on any particular bank, and by nightfall the vaults would be empty, the bank out of business. There were more than 11,000 such failures in the United States in the period 1929–33.

The people queuing outside this bank in New York want to withdraw their deposits. The bank is in the hands of the State Examiner, and is closed for 24 hours.

In addition, the banks demanded repayment of loans. People who had borrowed money to buy their homes, and businessmen who had borrowed money to start up a new business or expand an existing one, suddenly found their homes repossessed or their businesses **bankrupt**.

Chain reaction

All this was happening to an economy which had been slowing down even before the stock market crashed. In many industries and in farming there had already been too much production, and now the gap between what people could buy and what was being made widened at breakneck speed. Businesses in difficulty laid off workers, swelling the growing army of the unemployed. With fewer wages coming in, people spent less on goods, which put more businesses in difficulties and created even more unemployment. Those still in work were often forced to accept lower wages, which meant they could not buy as much in the shops as before.

The American economy seemed caught in a downward spiral. Between 1929 and the end of 1932 investment fell by half, industrial production fell by 43 per cent, and the total value of stocks by around 80 per cent. Unemployment rose to 25 per cent at its peak in 1933: one out of every four people was out of work. At one point in 1932 the jobless total was going up by 12,000 people each day. That year there were 23,000 suicides, the worst such year in American history.

> ### Borrowed time
>
> After two years the jazz age seems as far away as the days before the War. It was borrowed time anyhow – the whole upper tenth of a nation living with the insouciance [lack of concern] of grand dukes and the casualness of chorus girls.
>
> The American author F. Scott Fitzgerald, 1931

President Hoover at his desk in the White House. Hoover believed the economy would sort itself out.

The failure of government

The government and the business leaders did little to put things right. President Hoover thought the economy would sort itself out, and that intervention would do more harm than good. Business leaders promised to keep up wages, prices, investment and employment levels, and so halt the slide, but they failed to do this. Each company acted in its own interests. With the government unwilling to intervene there was no one to enforce the interests of the whole country.

When persuasion failed, the government did nothing. It would neither act to right the situation nor help those suffering the consequences. Hoover refused to consider relief payments to either the farmers or the millions of unemployed. He preferred clinging to the belief that a new period of prosperity was just around the corner.

From America to the rest of the world

Not all the losses on **Wall Street** had been American. As **share** prices had risen, many European financial institutions, such as banks, had been unable to resist such sensational profits, and they too suffered badly in the Great Crash. This would have been serious in itself for Europe and the rest of the world. The fact that the world economy had been set up like a row of dominoes by the post-war economic arrangements made things even worse.

Free food was distributed to the poor in Austria.

Europe ...

Germany was the first domino to fall. It had borrowed huge sums of money from the USA to finance its own economic recovery and the payment of **reparations** to Britain and France. Over half of these were short-term loans, which had to be renewed every few months. After the Great Crash, American banks, desperate to survive, simply demanded their money back. All over Germany companies either cut back or went **bankrupt**, and unemployment began remorselessly rising, from 1.32 million in September 1929 to 6.1 million in January 1933.

This was bad news for Britain and France in many ways. The crisis in Germany meant popular support increased for the extremist parties: the **communists** and Adolf Hitler's **Nazi** Party. Germany ended her reparations payments. President Hoover rubbed salt in this wound by refusing to cancel the British and French war debts to America.

Like business leaders in America, the world's most powerful governments seemed incapable of seeing beyond their own short-term interests, when their long-term interests would have been much better served by working together. For example, as the months went by they all started raising existing **tariffs** to protect their own industries. This soon led to a reduction in world trade, making matters worse for everybody.

Britain, as a trading nation, suffered more than most from this. The number of unemployed, which had been above a million since the war, rose considerably. France, which had a more rural economy, was less affected at first, but here too the jobless total moved upwards. It was the same story all over Europe – as **credit** became harder and harder to get, as the world economy shrank and businesses failed, the streets filled with people made idle through no fault of their own.

... and beyond

In the rest of the world it was the falling price of **primary products** which did most of the damage. Many of these prices were already falling before the Great Crash due to world-wide over-production, but the shrinking of the world economy sent them plummeting. Every nation which relied on selling such goods suffered.

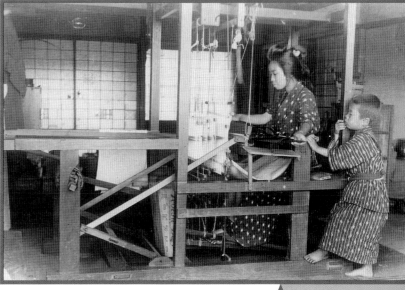

In Australia the price of wheat and wool fell by around 55 per cent between 1928 and 1931, and a severe drought in 1929 made matters worse. The total value of Australia's exports was almost halved during these few years. The collapse in 1930 of the American demand for Japanese silk caused great hardship in the Japanese countryside, and countries like Brazil, Ceylon and Cuba were hit by falling world prices for coffee, tea and sugar.

A Japanese silk weaver in 1938. Almost half of Japan's farmers relied on silk production to supplement their low income from other crops.

As these industries suffered, so the knock-on effect was felt throughout the economy. A small farmer in a far corner of India, pleading with his village moneylender for more time to pay his debts, probably had no idea that a world credit shortage was responsible for his moneylender's unusual refusal to take payment in crops. He would doubtless have had a hard time believing that his own struggle to make ends meet had suddenly grown more difficult because a few people had been overcome with gambling fever in lands beyond his horizon.

In the cities

For most ordinary people the central reality of the Great Depression was unemployment. Millions were unemployed or dependent on those who were, millions more were afraid of being so. In 1930 few countries paid any **benefits** to the unemployed, and those that were paid were often pitifully inadequate. Millions of people had to rely on charity, either in the form of relief pay-outs from governments – which often had humiliating conditions attached to them – or in the form of food and other necessary items distributed by the charity organizations.

Growing up in a Hooverville shanty town in Washington DC in 1932.

Homeless

Without wages, many people found it impossible to afford rents or **mortgage** payments, and were thrown out of their homes. All over the world shanty towns sprang up on empty sites, full of makeshift homes made from whatever materials the homeless could find. Others had no roof at all. In the summer of 1931 several hundred women slept each night in Chicago's parks. Fifty-four men, arrested for sleeping in a New York subway, were overjoyed to find that the police were too busy to process them. In jail they would receive several good meals and a decent bed for the night.

Many of the homeless abandoned their home towns and cities, taking to the road in the hope of finding a job elsewhere.

One young couple

*Attracted by smoke from the chimney of a supposedly empty summer cottage near Awana Lake, Constable Simon Glaser found a young couple starving. After three days without food, the wife, who is twenty-three years old, was hardly able to walk. The couple had been unemployed since their formerly wealthy employer lost his money, and several days ago they **invested** all they had, except 25 cents for food, in bus fare to this region in search of work. Finding none, they went to the cottage, preferring to starve rather than beg. They said they had resigned themselves to dying together.*

Report in the *New York Times*, Christmas Day 1931

In 1932 there were over 25,000 American families and some 200,000 young men wandering around the country in this way, spending their nights in railroad carriages, campsites and municipal shelters. In Australia, such transients were called 'soldiers of despair'.

Hungry

Many people spent a lot of their time hungry. In New York City, which had better relief services than most, one in five children was suffering from **malnutrition** in 1932. Newspapers published recipes using the cheapest ingredients, but many people could not afford even those. There were long queues for the bread and soup which were given out by the charity organizations, and in the worst areas people scrambled around in gutters and rubbish heaps looking for scraps of food.

Angry

In the face of such a human calamity, it was only natural that those who found themselves badly affected should feel angry. As the months went by, with no sign that matters were improving, ordinary people expressed this anger however they could. Most blamed their governments, and these, whether politically of the right or left, had a hard job holding on to power. In the USA President Hoover became so identified with the Depression that he lost any real chance of winning the next election. The shanty towns of the unemployed became known as 'Hoovervilles', and the food dished out in soup kitchens as 'Hoover stew'.

Unemployed workers eating a meal in a Chicago soup kitchen, 1930.

Protest

Fighting back

Protests often went far beyond name-calling. People all over the world were prepared to break the law if their own and their families' survival depended on it. Groups of the unemployed would often attack grocery stores, grabbing what they could from the shelves before the police turned up. Crowds would surround representatives of the authorities when they arrived at a particular home to cut off services, take back goods or evict the occupants. Often there would be violence, but sometimes events would take a comic turn, as protesters returned through the back door those items which the representatives of the authorities had removed through the front. As time went by neighbourhoods grew more organized, and 'Unemployed Councils' were formed to help those in need, supplying everything from new shoes to legal advice.

There was also increasing trouble at workplaces, and on many occasions this turned to violence. In the summer of 1931, in the American coalfields of Ohio, Pennsylvania and Kentucky, the owners used private armies to set up a reign of terror against the angry workers. In Dearborn, Michigan, in March 1932 four men were shot dead during a demonstration. Business and government leaders feared that the whole industrial situation could get out of hand, and many of them would later support President Roosevelt's answer to the crisis – the New Deal – because they feared that the only alternative was a revolution.

Soldiers of the 'Bonus Army' camped out in sight of the Capitol, Washington DC, 1932.

The Bonus Army

In the USA, the most famous demonstration was that mounted by the 'Bonus Army' in Washington. This 'army' was composed of World War One veterans who had, after that war, been promised a financial bonus in far-off 1945. By 1932 many of them were so poor that they asked for the payment to be brought forward. More than 20,000 veterans made their way to Washington, some even hijacking trains to complete their journey.

In June 1932 they set up a 'Hooverville' (shanty town) within sight of the White House, and demanded that **Congress** pay out their bonuses. When Congress refused to pay they refused to leave, and President Hoover decided to evict them.

Four troops of cavalry, four companies of infantry, a machine-gun squadron and six tanks were assembled near the White House, and then used to clear and destroy the veterans' camp. Three of the US Army officers involved – Douglas MacArthur, Dwight Eisenhower and George Patton – would later play prominent roles in World War Two.

The Jarrow March

In Great Britain the best-known demonstration of the time was a peaceful one. In the north-eastern town of Jarrow the closure of industries had left four out of five men without work, and in the autumn of 1936 several hundred of the unemployed walked the 300 miles to London to ask the government to create more jobs. The 'Jarrow Marchers' received much sympathy from the general population, but little more than empty promises of help from the authorities.

The Jarrow Marchers pass through a small English town.

In the USA and Britain the **democratic** political systems, with some minor changes, survived this rising tide of protest, and the revolution feared by a few failed to materialize. In other countries the banner of protest was carried by more extremist political groups, such as the **Nazis**, and when these came to power the changes would be more fundamental and far more dangerous.

Jarrow

Wherever we went there were men hanging about, not scores of them but hundreds and hundreds of them. The men wore the drawn masks of prisoners of war. A stranger from a distant civilization, observing the condition of the place and its people, would have arrived at once at the conclusion that Jarrow had deeply offended some celestial Emperor of the island and was now being punished.

The English writer J. B. Priestley, after a visit to Jarrow

On the land

A world problem

In most countries during the Great Depression life in the countryside was as difficult as life in the cities. Times had been hard since World War One. New technology had encouraged greater production, but since demand had not risen at the same rate, prices for most crops had started to fall. In order to maintain their income farmers had produced even more, but this of course brought the prices down still further. It grew much harder to export the extra crops because each country raised its import taxes to protect its own farmers.

An American farmer pours away milk that he cannot sell at a profit.

Many were forced to borrow money, but as prices kept falling it grew harder to keep up with repayments. During the Great Depression few banks could afford to wait for their money. As a result one in twenty American farmers lost their farms between 1930 and 1933. In some places, like Iowa, in the mid-west, the proportion was as high as one in eight.

Tenant farmers were even worse off. They often relied on their landlords to keep them during the winter; the following summer they would pay them back in crops. However, as the Depression took hold, and the crops came to be worth less and less, landlords became unwilling to support their tenants in this way. Many tenant farmer families took to the road and some starved, even in the United States.

Different responses

In some areas farmers tried to take matters into their own hands. In Iowa members of the local Farmers Union blocked roads and attacked trucks carrying food to the town. They hoped that by creating shortages they would drive up prices. As in the cities, people quickly gathered to try and prevent friends from being evicted.

Some simply gave way to despair. One American sheep farmer found that it would cost him $1.10 to ship each of his 3000 sheep to the market. He would receive only $1 per sheep in return. Rather than watch them starve he cut their throats and threw them in a canyon.

The situation was similar in all the countries which had relied on exporting agricultural products. As prices fell, crops were often left to wither in the fields because it cost more to harvest and transport them than they were worth. Farmers tried to cut costs by reverting to old ways of working – in Australia for example, horses were brought back to replace tractors, and the use of chemical fertilizers was drastically cut back.

A dustbowl farm in Colorado, USA. Its occupants have not yet joined the exodus to California.

The American dustbowls

In the United States several years of poor climatic conditions on the Great Plains made the situation still worse. Pockets of drought in 1930–1 spread further in 1932 and intensified in 1933. By 1934 a huge area covering a dozen states was affected. The **topsoil**, which had been held firm by the long grasses for thousands of years, had been exposed in the 1920s by over-cultivation and over-grazing, and now, dried out by the drought, it simply blew away, leaving 'dustbowls' where farming land had been.

The dustbowls were not caused by the Great Depression, but the streams of **migrants** heading north and west to escape it have become one of the most enduring images of the time. The hardships they went through, as told so movingly in John Steinbeck's novel *The Grapes of Wrath*, were certainly made much worse by the wider Depression affecting America as a whole.

A sin and a crime

And a homeless hungry man, driving the road with his wife beside him and his thin children in the back seat, could look at the fallow [uncultivated] fields which might produce food but not profit, and that man could know how a fallow field is a sin and the unused land a crime against thin children ...

And in the south he saw the golden oranges hanging on the trees, the little golden oranges on the dark green trees; and guards with shotguns patrolling the lines so a man might not pick an orange for a thin child, oranges to be dumped if the price was low ...

from *The Grapes of Wrath* by John Steinbeck

Roosevelt's New Deal

A new president

When the **Democratic Party's** Franklin Delano Roosevelt became president in March 1933, unemployment was still soaring and a collapse of confidence in the banks had led most of them to close their doors. Roosevelt acted decisively. There was relief money for the hungry and the homeless, and help with re-financing **mortgages** for those in danger of losing their houses and farms. To ensure that there was no repeat of the Great Crash, stricter regulations were introduced for banks and the **stock market**. Some accused him of behaving like a dictator, but most people were only too happy that at long last their government was doing something about the Depression.

By the end of summer 1933 300,000 CCC volunteers were engaged in a variety of tasks, like those here planting trees.

Getting America back to work

Before his election Roosevelt had promised 'a New Deal for the American people', and during 'the first hundred days' of his presidency he introduced a series of new laws to bring this about. The agencies created to see that these laws were enacted came to be known by their initials, and were called the 'Alphabet Agencies'.

The Civilian Conservation Corps (CCC) paid young men $1 a day to do public work. The new **Public Works** Administration (PWA) was formed to oversee the building of new houses, dams and hospitals, the electrification of railroads, and even the construction of a new sewage system for Chicago.

The PWA mostly employed skilled workers, but the Civil Works Administration (CWA) and the later Works Progress Administration (WPA) also took on unskilled labour. Some of the jobs they provided, like road-building and smartening up schools, were clearly useful, while others, like sweeping up leaves and researching strange subjects for no obvious reason, seemed less so. But for most of those involved, any sort of work was better than none.

There was also help for those who still had jobs. The National Recovery Administration (NRA) tried to set up codes of conduct in industry which would, eventually, benefit everybody. In return for giving its workers fair wages and the right to join unions, companies could use the NRA's symbol – a blue eagle with the motto 'we do our part' – as part of their advertising campaigns. In the countryside the Agricultural Adjustment Act (AAA) let the government pay farmers to produce less. This gave them a basic income and pushed up prices.

As part of the New Deal, the Tennessee Valley Authority generated thousands of jobs including building 21 dams.

The TVA

The most famous of the 'Alphabet Agencies', which oversaw the biggest government project of the entire New Deal, was the TVA, or Tennessee Valley Authority. The large area drained by the Tennessee River, which covered several states, had already been identified by Roosevelt as 'the nation's number one economic problem.' The TVA, by building 21 large dams and starting a massive **reafforestation** programme, would prevent the annual floods, help conserve the vanishing **topsoil** and generate enormous amounts of **hydroelectric power**.

Many of the measures introduced in 1933 had their limitations. The AAA–sponsored destruction of crops helped many farmers, but it greatly angered the hungry and did nothing for those farm workers who didn't own land. The public works programmes provided some jobs, but unemployment would remain high for many years. The system as a whole was not changed.

The overall effect was, however, positive. People had more money to spend, and the economy began to grow again. After four terrible years it seemed as if America was finally on the mend.

A letter to Roosevelt

Dear Mr President,
*   This is just to tell you that everything is all right now. The man you sent found our house all right and we went down the bank with him and the mortgage can go on a while longer. You remember I wrote about losing the furniture too. Well, your man got it back for us. I never heard of a president like you, Mr Roosevelt. Mrs ... and I are old folks and don't amount to much, but we are joined with those millions of others in praying for you every night. God bless you, Mr Roosevelt.*
sent to the White House, 1934

Making the New Deal work

Though necessary, the measures President Roosevelt introduced in 1933 were a great shock to many Americans. The **federal** government had never intervened so directly in the country's economic and political life. There were those who thought Roosevelt should have gone even further – people like the Louisiana politician Huey Long and radio broadcaster Father Charles Coughlin – but most of the opposition to his New Deal came from those who believed that he had gone too far. These opponents believed that government should do as little as possible to interfere with the way the **free market** operated.

Although Roosevelt's policies were not popular with industrialists, most people appreciated his programmes.

Roosevelt v. The Supreme Court

Among Roosevelt's most prominent opponents were many industrialists who believed that too much power was being given to their employees. Men like Henry Ford refused to sign up with the NRA, and many of the bosses who did sign were inclined to pick and choose which parts of the agreement they carried out. These opponents were mostly the people who had benefited from the **Republicans**' pro-business policies in the 1920s, and they still had support in **Congress** and the Supreme Court. When a New York company was accused by the NRA of selling diseased chickens, it took the case all the way to the Supreme Court, which ruled in its favour. The federal government, the judges said, had no right to interfere in the poultry business.

This was the beginning of a long struggle between Roosevelt and his opponents. Over the next few years fourteen other cases were brought before the Supreme Court, and nine of them went against the President. The AAA was declared illegal on the grounds that the states, and not the federal government, should be giving help to the farmers. The federal government was only supposed to be responsible for business which affected all the states, the judges said. The whole New Deal seemed in danger of being undone.

A second New Deal

Roosevelt fought back by introducing a second wave of laws. These created agencies to replace those which the Supreme Court had declared illegal, and virtually amounted to a second New Deal. The Wagner Act, which succeeded the NRA, gave workers the right to join and form unions. The Soil Conservation Act, which replaced the AAA, allowed the federal government to use care of the environment as its excuse for supporting the farmers. The Social Security Act broke new ground, setting up national systems of pensions, help for the disabled and **unemployment insurance**. Never again, it was hoped, would Americans be reduced to the poverty of the Great Depression's early years.

Roosevelt guessed that, left to its own devices, the Supreme Court would probably decide that this second New Deal was no more legal than the first. He countered this threat with another, promising to pack the Court with new judges if there was any attempt to block his measures. As a result, there was none.

In 1937 he decided that the worst of the Depression was over, and cut federal spending. This decision, which coincided with a downturn in world trade, proved a serious mistake. Industrial production and the **stock market** fell sharply, and unemployment climbed back past the 10 million mark during 1938. People expressed their dissatisfaction by giving the Republicans a majority in that year's elections to Congress, a result which effectively closed the door on any further New Deal legislation. The Great Depression was no longer Great, but unemployment would remain high until the American economy was boosted by the outbreak and spread of a new World War.

This New Deal era poster celebrating the value of work, was issued by the Works Progress Administration.

Roosevelt's pledge

I see millions denied education, recreation and the opportunity to better their lot and the lot of their children. I see millions lacking the means to buy the products of farm and factory and by their poverty denying work and productiveness to many other millions. I see one third of the nation ill-housed, ill-clad and ill-nourished. It is not despair that I paint you in this picture. I paint it for you in hope – because the Nation proposes to paint it out.

from Roosevelt's second Inaugural Speech January 1937

Great Britain and France

The Depression in Britain

Britain's Labour Government was just as unwilling to intervene decisively in the economy as the **Republican** administration in the USA had been. Economists like John Maynard **Keynes**, who pleaded for a **public works** programme to stimulate the economy, were ignored. Instead, the British government persisted with traditional policies. If the nation's **budget was balanced**, its leaders claimed, the situation would right itself. If times were hard the country needed to tighten its belt, not go on a spending spree. In July 1931 a report recommended cutting unemployment **benefit** and other government expenditure. Keynes called it 'the most foolish document' he had ever read.

I KNOW 3 TRADES
I SPEAK 3 LANGUAGES
FOUGHT FOR 3 YEARS
HAVE 3 CHILDREN
AND NO WORK FOR
3 MONTHS
BUT I ONLY WANT
ONE JOB

Britain's situation was worsened by the end of German **reparations** payments and the spread of **protectionism**, following the introduction of higher American **tariffs** in 1930. The British government eventually retaliated, ceasing payments on its war debt to the USA and introducing higher tariffs of its own for non-empire trade. An imperial conference was held in Ottawa, Canada, in 1932 to promote free trade inside the British empire, but the different countries and colonies were all too busy safeguarding their own interests to agree on very much.

In Britain unemployment continued to rise. A new national government introduced cuts in benefits and other spending, and carried on trying to balance the budget, but with little effect. The Depression was felt everywhere, but a few regions – North-east England, Scotland's Clyde valley, South Wales and Lancashire – were the most badly hit. Here, there was much suffering, with whole towns like Jarrow often devastated by the closure of one large industry. But they were a long way from London and the government. In the rest of England stable wages and lower prices meant many people were actually better off in the 1930s.

The Depression in France

The Depression came more slowly to France. The economy was less dependent on trade than Britain's, there was less industry that could be affected, and the impact of rising unemployment could be softened for the local inhabitants by sending home the many workers who came from nearby countries. It was not until 1932–3 that the country was seriously affected.

When this happened, French governments tried to follow the same traditional policies as the British. Unfortunately their political system, based on **proportional representation**, made it harder for them to take unpopular action. No party could ever gain an absolute majority in the French Parliament, and so government quickly followed government, with none able to really tackle the economic situation. The reputation of government itself was damaged, and there was growing support for extremist parties of both left and right. By the end of the 1930s France was a deeply divided nation.

The political consequences

There was no New Deal before World War Two in either Britain or France. This was partly because there was less need for one – social benefits were already better in these countries than in the United States – but more because of the political culture. Britain's backward-looking political parties had no sense of adventure, and the French political system made it virtually impossible for any party to push through such a daring programme of change.

Striking French workers from the north on a hunger march in 1933.

The economies of both countries were eventually stimulated back into growth by **rearmament** programmes and the general recovery of the world economy. But the absence of anything resembling a New Deal reflected a lack of confidence in the political leaderships of both countries, and this would have a disastrous effect on their dealings with a Germany that was rising up again.

The colonial world

In the 1930s most of the world beyond Europe and North America was still ruled by a few European countries. Even those countries in Africa, Asia and Latin America not ruled, directly or indirectly, by one of these European powers had little real independence in economic matters. When it came to trade they were **colonies** in everything but name.

These countries and colonies sold food and raw materials to Europe and North America, and used the money they received to buy manufactured goods. Until the end of World War One this seemed a reasonably fair arrangement, but in the 1920s the price of food and raw materials fell in relation to the price of industrial goods. With the onset of the Great Depression this gap grew even wider, pushing the interests of the trading partners further and further apart.

A riot in Melbourne, December 1933.

Australia

Australia's situation was typical. Wool and wheat prices fell. The economy shrank. Unemployment soared. Men marched, shanty towns went up, violence erupted. As elsewhere, some people prospered amidst the general gloom.

Because the economy was so entangled with that of Britain, the government was forced to follow the same mistaken policies of wage reduction and spending cuts. The worst was over by 1933, and there was even compensation in the fact that new industries had sprung up to produce those goods which the country could no longer afford to import. The Great Depression made Australians eager to assert their economic independence, and more capable of being so.

On instructions from owners, estate agents had been throwing bankrupt people out of their homes. People took the law into their own hands in retaliation:

It was late shopping night and at a quarter to nine there were two of us outside each of nine estate agents in Richmond. One chap in each group had a watch and they were all synchronized. At a quarter to nine, 'Bang!' We wrecked every estate agent's window in Richmond with lumps of bluemetal. There was hell to pay the next morning. The papers were full of it.

A member of the Unemployed Workers Movement in Richmond, Australia

India, Africa and Latin America

India was still a British colony, and its economy was run by the colonial power. When British and Indian interests differed, there was no doubt as to whose would come first. At the Ottawa Conference 10 Indian products were given **preferential access** to the British market, 162 British products similar access to the Indian market. In India itself, the British simply tried to **balance the budget**, as they had at home. There was no help for the rich farmers, landlords and money-lenders who had been hit by the Great Depression, and from this time on many would join the vast ranks of the poor in supporting the Indian Congress Party and its struggle for independence.

In Africa the Depression was first felt in those sectors of the economy – the mines, plantations and **cash-crop** areas – which were most closely linked to the colonial homelands in Europe. Banks cut back on their operations, companies cut wages and sacked workers. The prices paid to growers plummeted. As the continent's people had less money to spend, so the whole economy shrank, leaving only **subsistence farmers** unaffected. European enterprises were hit by a rise in the number of strikes, and there were boycotts of foreign stores.

The same economic processes occurred in Latin America, where most nations were at least in theory independent. But in matters of trade their governments were as powerless as local colonial administrations, and much more vulnerable to popular discontent. In Brazil and Argentina regimes which had been in power since World War One were toppled by Depression discontent.

All over the world beyond Europe and North America there was disillusion with a colonial system which had so obviously failed to protect its peoples from the impact of the Great Depression. This disillusion would provide the fuel for the numerous independence movements which sprang into existence during and after World War Two.

Mahatma Gandhi (on the left) and other leaders of the Indian Congress Party leadership, 1938.

Germany and Japan

The rise of the Nazis

In Germany, throughout the period 1930–2, a succession of governments tried to deal with the worsening economic situation in much the same way as the British and French. They cut services, **benefits** and wages, trying to **balance the budget**. When these policies failed, the German people, who had already suffered extreme hardships in the 1920s, showed that they were prepared to take desperate measures. As unemployment went up so did the number of votes cast for Hitler's **Nazi** Party.

Hitler blamed foreigners for Germany's plight, the western powers for imposing such a harsh peace in 1918, and the Jews within Germany, who he wrongly claimed were manipulating the economy for their own selfish ends. In the July 1932 elections the Nazis won more votes than any other party, and in January 1933 Hitler became Chancellor, the leader of the German government. By mid-1934 he had effectively turned Germany from a **democracy** into a **dictatorship**.

Hitler's economic success

More by luck than judgement, the Nazis adopted economic policies which proved successful in dealing with the Depression in Germany. Since they wanted their control over the country to be complete, they were much more willing to intervene directly in the economy than the British or French. They were also determined to restore German pride and military strength, which involved spending a lot of public money on the construction of the motorways and a **rearmament** programme. This high spending soon got the German economy moving again. Hitler quickly pointed out that his party had succeeded where his predecessors, and Britain and France, had failed. German pride had been restored, while the reputation of democracy was further damaged.

Hitler opened the first stretch of the motorway between Frankfurt am Main and Darmstadt, 19 May 1935.

All that seemed to stand between Germany and a full recovery from her post-war troubles was the settlement imposed by the **Treaty of Versailles**. Hitler's economic successes won him the support he needed at home to start to undo that settlement. His massive rearmament programme would eventually give him the means to break it by force.

Japanese answers

The Japanese had also been hard hit by the Depression, especially in the countryside, where the dramatic slump in the world silk and rice markets created areas of desperate poverty. Between 1929 and 1931 the Japanese government followed the British, French and Germans in pursuing traditional policies, with much the same results, but in late 1931 a new Minister of Finance, Takahashi Korekiyo, introduced similar policies to those which **Keynes** had recommended in Britain. The Japanese currency was allowed to fall in value, helping Japanese companies, initially at least, to sell more abroad. Public spending was increased, which put money in people's pockets, and so allowed Japanese companies to sell more at home. The economy began to grow again.

Unfortunately, the damage done to the countryside in 1929–31 had already had political consequences. The worst-hit areas were some of the army's main recruiting areas, and many of the men were outraged by the government's inability to improve matters. The armed forces were responsible to the emperor, not the government, allowing them to have their own policies. Their answer to the Depression, in the summer of 1931, was to complete the invasion of China's Manchuria and turn it into a virtual Japanese colony. With a single stroke, or so the army leaders claimed, they had created a new market for Japanese industry and extra room for the rapidly-growing Japanese population.

These two policies – the army's invasion of Manchuria and the government's promotion of exports – both helped to sour Japan's relations with the other rich countries. Condemned for the invasion of Manchuria, Japan left the **League of Nations**. Other nations raised **tariffs** higher and higher in an attempt to keep out her **exports**. By the mid-1930s Japan's only friends seemed to be Germany and Italy.

> ## Method in his madness
>
> *There can be no flourishing economic life which has not before it and behind it a flourishing, powerful State as its protection ... There can be no economic life unless behind this economic life there stands the determined political will of the nation absolutely ready to strike, and to strike hard ...*
>
> Adolf Hitler, January 1932

A Japanese army column marches through a Manchurian town during the invasion of 1931.

Race and gender

The Great Depression had an undeniable impact on how particular groups saw themselves and each other.

Racism in Europe

When times are hard they tend to be hardest for minorities, and this was certainly true in many areas during the Depression. Hitler claimed that the Jews were largely responsible for Germany's economic problems, and in 1935 his Nuremberg Laws stripped all German Jews of their citizenship and prohibited interracial marriages. This persecution would intensify as the years passed, and culminate in the obscenity of the **Holocaust**.

*Anti-Jewish placards in the window of a Berlin store during a **boycott** of Jewish goods in **Nazi** Germany, 1933.*

The Germans were the most violent culprits, but far from the only ones. The Jews were used as convenient **scapegoats** throughout central and eastern Europe. In western countries like France, workers from eastern and southern Europe were much more likely to find themselves losing their jobs than those born in the area. The seriousness of such discrimination varied enormously from place to place. The British Union of **Fascists** tried hard to stir up racial hatred against the Jews in England, but with little success.

African-Americans

The 1930s offered a mixed message to African-Americans. As a whole they suffered badly from the Depression. When companies shed jobs they were often the first to be fired, and the white-run unions frequently ignored them. As **tenant farmers** or domestic workers they didn't qualify for farm **subsidies** or unemployment **benefits**. There was no new anti-**lynching** law, and many states still had laws discriminating against them.

Large parts of American life, like sports and the armed services, were still **segregated**. African-American neighbourhoods in big cities were over-crowded and very poor. In March 1935 rioters in Harlem – the ghetto in New York City – set out to destroy the local white-owned businesses.

There was some good news. President Roosevelt was reluctant to risk upsetting white voters by supporting African-American causes, but he did argue in favour of an anti-lynching bill. His wife Eleanor frequently

Not like home

*Europe is a different world.
You can go anywhere, do
anything, talk to anybody.
You can't believe it.*

African-American trumpeter
Rex Stewart, on tour with
Duke Ellington in 1939

spoke out against the evils of
racial discrimination. More
significantly, it was written into
New Deal programmes that they
had to be applied in a **non-discriminatory** manner. Some historians
have considered this an early step along the road to **civil rights**.

*An African-
American
family in a
Washington
slum, 1937.*

Women

On the whole, most women's lives barely changed from the 1920s to
the 1930s. They looked after the children and home, and in many
poorer countries they did most of the work in the fields as well.

In the richer countries the 1920s had seen a change in many women's
expectations. This was reflected in many different ways, from voting
rights to smoking in public. In the United States and western Europe
women were starting to claim equal rights in all sorts of areas. Partly in
reaction to this, partly in reaction to the new circumstances of the
Great Depression, the 1930s was a period of marking time where
women's rights were concerned. Many women lost their jobs and their
financial independence. Those in work often had to suffer the mocking
accusations of those who said they were taking a man's job away.

There was a shift back towards the belief that a woman's place was in
the home, particularly in Germany. This trend was reinforced by another
peculiarity of the 1930s – the new emphasis on home life for all the
family, which accompanied the heyday of radio and the introduction of
so many new household appliances, such as fridges and vacuum cleaners.
Women who could afford such labour-saving devices certainly found
housework easier than their mothers had done, but in the world beyond
their front door there was little to cheer. Equality of pay, work and
opportunity often looked further away in the 1930s than it had during
the giddy optimism of the 1920s.

Arts and entertainment

The Great Depression influenced the development of mass entertainment and the arts in many, often contradictory, ways. Entertainments which allowed people to 'escape' their problems for a while became popular, while the more adventurous arts were often held back by a lack of funds. Telling the stories of those caught up in the real-life Depression inspired some powerful music, novels and films.

In the USA, one New Deal agency, the WPA, gave money to all sorts of artists as part of its job creation programme. Thousands of actors and musicians travelled across the country putting on plays and concerts, often for people who had rarely seen either before. Writers were paid to write plays for the theatre groups and practical books like tourist guides to American states and cities. Painters decorated public buildings with murals and held exhibitions in schools. Photographers were employed to keep a record of life during the Depression. The historian Howard Zinn called this 'an exciting flowering of arts for the people', and though the **subsidies** were withdrawn in 1939, many lives had been enriched.

Henry Fonda (centre) as Tom Joad in John Ford's film of The Grapes of Wrath, *based on Steinbeck's novel.*

From the 1920s to the 1930s

The thirties weren't easy for innovators. The twenties in America had produced a golden era of jazz, several ground-breaking novelists, and the 'Harlem renaissance' of African-American writers and musicians. Legendary artists like F. Scott Fitzgerald, William Faulkner, Langston Hughes, Bessie Smith, George Gershwin, Duke Ellington, Louis Armstrong and Hoagy Carmichael had all come to prominence. But in the thirties improvisational jazz did not advance, there were few great new novelists, and the 'Harlem renaissance' faded.

The new golden era was Hollywood's. Through the years of the Great Depression American film stars became household names throughout the world. Other countries had film industries, but none could compete with the 'Dream Factory' for volume and popularity. In cinemas across the planet people sat entranced by films which offered a picture of the way life should be, rather than the way it was in the grim depths of the Depression.

Mass spectator sports shared this boom in 'escapist' entertainment, but this industry grew mostly within national boundaries. Few Europeans had heard of baseball's Babe Ruth, and even fewer Americans would have recognized the name of cricket's Don Bradman, though both could claim to be the finest in their game's history.

Singer/song-writer Woodie Guthrie's 'dustbowl ballads' portrayed the life of the poor.

Telling it like it was

Many writers did try to come to terms with the Great Depression, and their works offer a vivid picture of ordinary life in this period. Britain's George Orwell chronicled the era in two novels: *Down and Out in Paris and London* and *The Road to Wigan Pier*. The French writer Louis-Ferdinand Céline covered much the same ground in his *Journey to the End of the Night*. John Steinbeck's novel *The Grapes of Wrath*, which was also filmed by director John Ford, is a harrowing account of one family's journey across America, from their dust-destroyed farm on the Great Plains to an equally difficult life as migrant fruit pickers in California. Woody Guthrie, the other American artist most associated with the Depression, put the stories of such families into a series of songs, which became known as 'the dustbowl ballads.' Steinbeck and Guthrie were both angry and accusing, but they also offered much more – a portrait of how rich and wonderful life could be, even for those who seemed to have so little.

> *Now as through the world I ramble,*
> *I see lots of funny men,*
> *Some will rob you with a six-gun,*
> *and some with a fountain pen.*
>
> *But as through this life you travel,*
> *And as through your life you roam,*
> *You won't never see an outlaw*
> *Drive a family from their home.*
> from Woody Guthrie's song *Pretty Boy Floyd*

> *You discover what it is like to be hungry. With bread and margarine in your belly you go out and look into the shop windows. Everywhere there is food insulting you in huge wasteful piles …*
> George Orwell in his 1930s reminiscences *Down and Out in Paris and London*

Economics and politics

Keynesianism

If one man came out of the Great Depression with his reputation enhanced it was the English economist John Maynard **Keynes**. He had been right in 1919 when he said that **reparations** would do more harm than good, right again in 1931 when he said that traditional, budget-balancing policies would make the situation worse. Those countries which, through accident or design, followed the economic policies which he recommended were the first to emerge from the Depression.

The English economist John Maynard Keynes, who consistently argued for government intervention in the economy.

Keynes outlined his theories in a series of books: *The Economic Consequences of the Peace* (1919), *A Treatise on Money* (1930) and, most important of all, *The General Theory of Employment, Interest and Money* (1936). His central idea was that in the modern age, economies were not self-regulating. Governments needed to intervene – to manage them, to learn how to use the controls at their disposal to keep them functioning at the best possible level. In times of depression they could start **public works** or have lower taxes, either of which would pump more **demand** into the economy (people would want to buy and spend), and so get it moving again. And, if the economy was over-heating and **inflation** accelerating, they could slow it down by cutting back demand, taking the money out of people's pockets in higher taxes or higher **interest rates**.

Both Roosevelt's New Deal and Hitler's recovery plan for Germany involved the injection of public money to stimulate the economy, but such measures were seen as an emergency response to the Depression, not as a normal economic way of life. It was not until 1944 that Keynes's ideas would become the official policy of his own country. Most other countries would also adopt them in the post-war era.

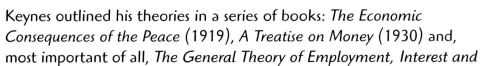

How economies work

*If the Treasury were to fill old bottles with banknotes, bury them at suitable depths in disused coal mines which are then filled up to the surface with town rubbish, and leave it to **private enterprise** [businesses not under state control] on well-tried principles of **laissez-faire** to dig the notes up again ... there need be no more unemployment and, with the help of the repercussions, the real income of the community ... would probably become a good deal larger than it actually is.*

J. M. Keynes, demonstrating that almost any government expenditure will create jobs and generate wealth, in his *General Theory of Employment, Book III*

Soviet planning

The levels of government intervention recommended by Keynes were considered 'socialistic' by many, and with good reason. **Socialists** of all kinds had long argued for this, although they were usually more interested in promoting greater equality than the overall health of the economy. The Union of Soviet Socialist Republics, or Soviet Union, had taken this intervention to its logical extreme. Its political leaders and economic planners had assumed direct control of almost all economic activity, allowing very little free play for **market forces**.

When it became clear that interventionist policies were succeeding in fighting the Great Depression, many people in Europe and America looked to the experience of the Soviet Union with more interest. That country was affected by the collapse of world raw material prices which characterized the Depression, but its economy seemed to carry on growing regardless. There was no unemployment, no spread of shanty towns, no apparent despair.

The Soviet Union protected its economy by implementing Five-Year Plans.

How had the Soviet Union made itself immune to this economic virus which had incapacitated everyone else? Many began to wonder if the Soviet Union's Five-Year Plans were the answer. They seemed to make more sense than just leaving things to take care of themselves.

This was an understandable view. Security of employment, in particular, looked wonderful to those millions in the West who had been thrown out of work through no fault of their own. But it was also a very partial view. It would be years before most people outside the Soviet Union realized this. The truth was that such levels of government intervention always seemed to go hand in hand with both growing economic inefficiency and a gross neglect of other human rights.

Short-term effects: the drift to war

The Great Depression did not inevitably lead to World War Two, but its consequences certainly made conflict more likely. The period of intense economic hardship gave birth to nationalistic and militaristic governments in Germany, Japan and most of the countries of eastern Europe. These governments created an atmosphere of confrontation both inside and outside their own countries, and deliberately brought those national grievances which had been left simmering since the Versailles settlement of 1919 back to the boil. This was particularly true of Germany, where both the **Nazis** and the military were determined to rewrite the settlement in their own favour.

With the military playing such a prominent role in these regimes, **rearmament** was a popular policy. It not only helped their economies out of Depression and made the new regimes more popular, but also made them more confident about getting their own way, particularly against weaker neighbours. When they succeeded in bullying one neighbour into submission, they were encouraged to try with another. This worried the other great powers, who began rearming themselves. Sooner or later someone was bound to make a stand, and then there would be war.

Adolf Hitler crossed into the Sudetenland region of Czechoslovakia, which had just been awarded to Germany at the Munich Conference.

Five economic blocs

The shrinking of the world economy made each nation anxious to protect – and, if possible, to expand – existing markets for their own industries. Protecting markets involved building ever-higher **tariff** barriers to other nations' goods. By about 1935 the world economy had become roughly divided into five economic blocs. These were the sterling area (the British empire, Scandinavia and parts of South America), the dollar area (North and Central America and parts of South America), the yen area (Japan and parts of China), the gold bloc (the French and Italian empires), and the Deutschmark area (Germany, central and eastern Europe).

The high tariff walls surrounding these blocs made it hard for any country to sell outside its own bloc. Most states found this difficult to accept, but Germany and Japan found it particularly annoying. They pointed out that the western powers already had their empires, so their need for new markets was not so desperate. They insisted that they too should be allowed to expand.

Preparing for war: the Krupp factory at Essen, Germany.

The Japanese expanded on the Asian mainland. They occupied Manchuria in 1931 and set out to conquer the rest of China in 1937. The Germans looked to eastern Europe, making a series of claims against Czechoslovakia and then Poland. Hitler's long-term aim was to find *lebensraum* – 'living space' – further east, in what was then the Soviet Union.

All these developments – the rise of **fascism**, the spread of rearmament, the creation of tariff blocs and the thrust to expand markets – were either caused by or quickened by the Great Depression. They all encouraged the spread of aggressive nationalism. The Depression even blunted the **League of Nations**' one weapon against aggressive behaviour. With everyone so desperate to sell, **economic sanctions** were impossible to enforce.

After World War Two

The western powers came to understand that the political and economic policies they had pursued in the 1920s and 1930s had been partly to blame for the conditions which led to the outbreak of World War Two, and after defeating Germany and Japan they tried to avoid repeating their past mistakes.

Dark times

What times are these when a conversation About trees is almost a crime. Because it includes a silence about so many misdeeds!

from German playwright Bertolt Brecht's poem *To Posterity*

There were no **reparations** to warp the post-war world economy, and the United States, rather than standing aloof as she had in 1918–19, took a leading role in the United Nations. Even more crucially, this time the Americans made sure that everyone would recover economically from the war and that no lasting grudges would be left to fester. Enormous amounts of money were poured into Europe and Japan, and the former enemies were soon readmitted to the prosperous family of nations.

Legacies of the Great Depression

The years of the Great Depression witnessed the greatest ever threat to the free enterprise or **capitalist** system. There were real fears of total collapse and revolution in the world's richest countries. World War Two brought an end to the Depression, but its effects are still being felt today. The changes it forced on governments did not vanish automatically when times improved, and the bitter memories of those who endured the greatest hardships were not wiped away by the steady growth of the post-war world. The legacy differed from continent to continent, but all were affected in some way.

One long-term consequence for the United States was the creation of the so-called 'Imperial Presidency'. In order to push through his economic and social policies, Roosevelt had stretched the power of the presidency and the **federal** government beyond previously accepted limits, and this trend continued during the war. In the second half of the century many Americans believed that their country had a president with too much power, and 'too much government' in general.

In western Europe the most obvious reaction to the economic competition of the 1930s, and the military war which followed, was a steady growth of cooperation in the economic and political arenas. The European Economic Community demolished the **tariff** walls between national states and ushered in a new era of relative harmony.

India celebrates independence from Britain, August 1947.

In Asia, Africa and Latin America the Depression had sown the seeds of discontent throughout Europe's overseas possessions, and the post-war world reaped the harvest. India and Indonesia became independent as early as the late 1940s, and by the end of the century only a few isolated outposts of the **colonial** empires remained.

The Soviet Union, which had seemed immune to the effects of the Depression, probably benefited from it. For many people it looked as if the Soviets had succeeded where **capitalism** had failed. The propaganda boost lasted for years. If the Great

Depression had not occurred it would have been harder to take Soviet **communism** seriously as an alternative method of running an economy.

Some consequences of the Depression affected everyone in the non-Soviet world. After the war it was generally believed that tariff walls between national states were bad for business and political harmony. The western powers set up GATT (the General Agreement on Tariffs and Trade) to promote **free trade**. There were problems with this. The richer countries insisted on protecting some industries against outside competition. The poorer countries were rightly worried about their chances of survival in a trading 'free-for-all'. Such issues continue to generate disputes to this day.

Dorothea Lange's famous photographs of migrant workers in California during the 1930s provide a moving pictorial record of the Great Depression.

The discrediting of laissez-faire

Inside national states the main legacy of the Depression was a distrust of do-nothing **laissez-faire** policies. For one thing, they didn't work. For another, they resulted in absurdities like the destruction of unsaleable food while people went hungry, and the closure of factories which made goods people wanted. Such things seemed more than absurd – they seemed fundamentally wrong. By the end of the 1930s the idea that economies ran themselves for the benefit of everyone had been almost completely discredited, and after the war governments were expected to intervene across the whole range of economic activities.

They took charge of the economic levers – things like tax and **interest rates**, money supply and government borrowing levels – and used them to shift economic activity in whatever direction seemed necessary at any given time. The job of governments was to make sure that the economy was working in everyone's interests, and to provide a whole range of social **benefit** payments for those – the elderly, the disabled, the unemployed – who through no fault of their own were prevented from playing a full part in the economic process.

Making the connection

We have always known that heedless self-interest was bad morals. We now know that it is bad economics.

President Roosevelt, Second Inaugural Address, January 1937

Great Depression timeline

1914 Beginning of World War One
1917 Russian Revolution
         USA enters the war
1918 End of World War One
1919 Treaty of Versailles
         Founding of the League of Nations
1921 Warren Harding becomes US president
         German reparations bill decided
1923 French occupation of the Ruhr, Germany
         The Great Inflation in Germany
         Warren Harding dies in office, succeeded by Calvin Coolidge
1924 The Dawes Plan
1926 General Strike in Britain
1928 Share prices soar on Wall Street, New York
1929 Herbert Hoover becomes president.
         The Great Crash on Wall Street
1930 Unemployment rises worldwide. Prices, trade and production
         fall
1931 Japanese invasion of Manchuria
         National government formed in Britain
1932 British empire conference in Ottawa, Canada
1933 Hitler comes to power in Germany
         Roosevelt becomes president
         First New Deal measures
1934 Dustbowl conditions on the American Great Plains
1935 Social Security Act in the USA
1937 Roosevelt's second inauguration
         New recession in the USA
         Japanese invasion of China
1938 Germany takes over Austria and part of Czechoslovakia
1939 Outbreak of World War Two
1945 End of World War Two
         Founding of the United Nations
1948 GATT formed
1957 Treaty of Rome sets up European Economic Community

Highs and lows – graphs

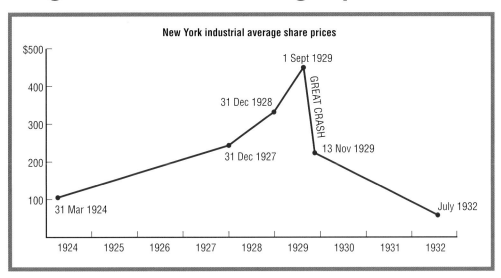

New York industrial average share prices

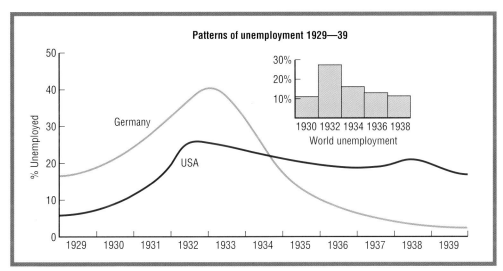

Patterns of unemployment 1929—39

Further reading

History books

Causes and Consequences of the Great Depression, Stuart Ross, Evans, 1997

Living Through History: Twentieth Century World, Nigel Kelly, Rosemary Rees and Jane Shuter, Heinemann Library, 1998

History of Britain: Modern Britain, Andrew Langley, Heinemann Library, 1994

History of America, The Rise to World Power, Sally Senzell Isaacs, Heinemann Library, 1999

The Great Depression, Marion Yass, Wayland, 1988

Sources

A New Deal, Josh Brooman, Longman, 1986

The Great Depression, David F. Burg, Facts on File, 1996

Hard Times, Studs Terkel, Pantheon, 1970

A People's History of the United States, Howard Zinn Longman, 1980

Novels

Down and Out in Paris and London, George Orwell, Secker, 1969

The Grapes of Wrath, John Steinbeck, Penguin, 1976

The Freedom Tree, James Watson, Puffin, 1998

Roll of Thunder, Hear My Cry, Mildred Taylor, Puffin, 1995

Great Depression website

www.bbc.co.uk/education/modern/crash/ crashhtm.htm

Glossary

balance the budget make sure that what a government spends does not exceed government income, or vice versa

bankrupt officially unable to pay debts

benefit payment made by a government to those who, for various reasons, are unable to work

boom period of sharp economic growth

boycott refusal to have any dealings with a business firm or other institution

broker professional buyer and seller of shares

capitalism free enterprise economic system, in which most business is privately owned and run

cash-crop crop grown for sale rather than consumption, often for export

civil rights rights of all people to the same equal opportunities and benefits

colony territory ruled by another, usually faraway, country

communism political system in which most property is owned by the state

Congress legislative body of the USA, which makes the laws. It comprises the Senate and the House of Representatives.

credit money available for borrowing

demand in economics, what is both wanted by people and affordable

democracy government by the people or their elected representatives

Democratic Party in the USA, one of the two major political parties, usually more in favour of government intervention in the economy than the Republicans

dictatorship government by individuals or small groups in which the mass of the people have no say

direct tax tax like income tax which takes more from the rich than the poor

economic sanctions refusal to trade with another nation, either in one particular product or in all

exports goods or services sold to other countries

fascism dictatorial system of government originating in Italy, which was later known for its aggressive nationalism. Nazism was one type of fascism.

federal the central government in the USA, based in Washington DC

free market market unregulated or little regulated by government

free trade trade without tariffs

Holocaust murder of six million Jews by Nazi Germany in 1942–5

hydroelectric power electricity generated by the power of water

imports goods or services bought from foreign countries

indirect tax tax which tends to penalize rich and poor by the same amount (which the rich can better afford)

inflation increase in prices or increase in the supply of money (which leads to an increase in prices)

interest rates levels at which borrowed money must be repaid

invest put money into economic projects, in the hope of making a profit

Keynes economist John Maynard Keynes proposed state control of the economy through taxes and the money supply

laissez-faire pure capitalism, without interference by governments

League of Nations international organization set up after World War One to help settle disputes between nations

lynching execution without legal trial

malnutrition lack of the food necessary for health

migrant someone with no fixed home address who travels in search of work

market forces the workings of supply (what is or is not available) and demand (what is or is not wanted)

mortgage loan taken out to buy a home or business property

Nazis the German National Socialists, led by Adolf Hitler

non-discriminatory applied in the same way to everyone

preferential access provision of lower tariffs for one nation's exports than another's

primary products raw materials like crops and minerals

private enterprise business not owned or controlled by government

propaganda promotion of ideas, often involving a selective version of the truth

proportional representation system of voting in which each party is represented in proportion to the votes it receives

protectionism use of tariffs to protect industry and agriculture from foreign competition

public works building operations organized and financed by the government

racism hatred of other races

reafforestation replanting with trees

rearmament increase in the production of weaponry

recession economic downturn

reparations payments to make amends for war damage

Republican Party in the USA, one of the two major political parties, usually less in favour of government intervention in the economy than the Democrats

scapegoat person blamed for other people's shortcomings

segregated kept apart. Often applied to ethnic groups, such as the black and white communities in the USA.

shares certificates which represent pieces of a business and which entitle the holders to a share of any profits (money the business makes after all the costs of running the business have been paid for)

socialism political system which puts more stress on the needs of the community as a whole and less on the needs of the individual

speculator person who makes money by gambling on changes in the price of stocks and shares

stock money loaned to a company or government in return for a share in the profits

stock market place where stocks and shares are bought and sold

subsidy extra money given, usually by government, to help out individuals or businesses

subsistence farmers farmers who grow food just for themselves and their families

tariffs charges for bringing goods across international borders

tenant farmers farmers who rent their farms

topsoil fertile top layer of soil

Treaty of Versailles formal list of arrangements forced on the defeated Germany at the end of World War One

trust company that buys and sells shares on behalf of individuals

unemployment insurance money paid out by government to the unemployed on a regular basis

Wall Street centre of New York's business district. Site of its Stock Exchange.

Index

Titles in the *20th Century Perspectives* series include:

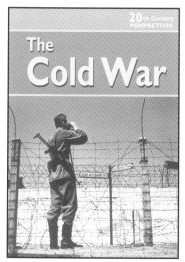

Hardback   0 431 11984 8

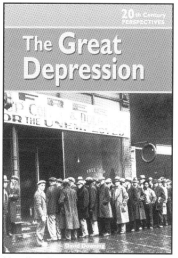

Hardback   0 431 11980 5

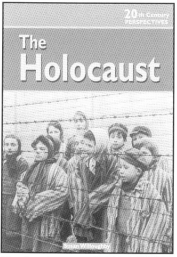

Hardback   0 431 11983 X

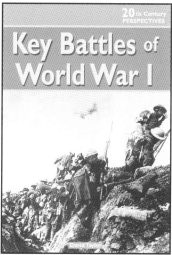

Hardback   0 431 11981 3

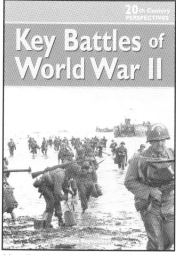

Hardback   0 431 11982 1

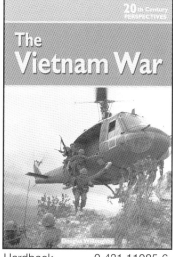

Hardback   0 431 11985 6

Find out about the other titles in this series on our website www.heinemann.co.uk/library

The Great
Depression

David Downing

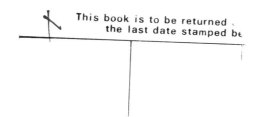

This book is to be returned
the last date stamped b

CLASS	BARCODE
338.542	R76815W
DATE	— 6 FEB 2002

www.heinemann.co.uk
Visit our website to find out more information about Heinemann Library books.

To order:
 Phone 44 (0) 1865 888066
 Send a fax to 44 (0) 1865 314091
🖥 Visit the Heinemann Bookshop at www.heinemann.co.uk to browse our catalogue and order online.

First published in Great Britain by Heinemann Library,
Halley Court, Jordan Hill, Oxford OX2 8EJ,
a division of Reed Educational and Professional Publishing Ltd.
Heinemann is a registered trademark of Reed Educational and Professional Publishing Ltd.

OXFORD MELBOURNE AUCKLAND
JOHANNESBURG BLANTYRE GABORONE
IBADAN PORTSMOUTH (NH) USA CHICAGO

Designed by AMR
Illustrated by Art Construction
Originated by Dot Gradations
Printed by Wing King Tong in Hong Kong.

ISBN 0431 11980 5
05 04 03 02 01
10 9 8 7 6 5 4 3 2 1

British Library Cataloguing in Publication Data
Downing, David,
   The Great Depression. – (20th century perspectives)
   1.Depressions – 1929 – Juvenile literature
   I.Title
   338.5'42'09042

Acknowledgements
The publishers would like to thank the following for permission to reproduce photographs:
Archive Photos/Frank Driggs, p.11; Corbis, pp.15, 16, 22, 27, 32, 37; Corbis/Bettmann, p.25; Corbis/UPI, p.14; David King, p.39; Hulton Getty, pp. 5, 4, 7, 8, 9, 10, 13, 17, 18,19, 20, 21, 23, 24, 26, 28, 29, 30, 31, 32, 33, 34, 36, 38, 40, 41, 42, 43; Imperial War Museum, p.6; The Library of Congress, pp.12, 35.

Cover photograph reproduced with permission of Corbis.

Our thanks to Christopher Gibb for his comments in the preparation of this book.

Every effort has been made to contact copyright holders of any material reproduced in this book. Any omissions will be rectified in subsequent printings if notice is given to the publishers.

Any words appearing in the text in bold, **like this**, are explained in the glossary.